CROCHET Shawls and Blankets

PO Box 152, Mill Hill, London NW7, England

First published in 1992

ISBN 0 7111 0016 0

Printed in Belgium by
Proost International Book Production

Introduction

HARMONY CLASS is for everyone. Beginners will find the classes friendly and instructional, experienced crocheters will find them challenging and informative.

The CROCHET CLASS brings you the possibility of crocheting your own individual shawl or blanket.

Step-by-step instructions for some of the most common techniques for working motifs are followed by the instructions for the classic Shawl.

The classic Shawl is the basis for all the variations that can be made by using the other motifs given. The third section gives you a selection of different motifs that you can put together to in lots of different ways. We have included some suggested combinations to inspire you but do plan your own designs - your only limitation being whether it is possible to fit your planned design into the desired width of the finished item! Remember - **the choice is yours**.

Basic crochet techniques which will be of particular interest to the less experienced crocheter follow, and we finish with some hints and tips which could be helpful to all of you.

Incidentally, we would be glad to hear from **you** if you have tips which we can add to future editions of our books and which would interest other crocheters.

Contents

Crochet

About Crochet

Traditionally crochet was worked almost exclusively in very fine cotton yarn to create or embellish household items such as curtains, table cloths or place mats. With the increase in the availability of yarn in a wide variety of textures and colours we are no longer limited to just these articles when we consider ways to use the craft of crochet.

Motifs

Working in Rounds

Most motifs are not worked to and fro in rows but from the centre outwards in rounds. Unless otherwise indicated do not turn the work between rounds but continue with the same side facing and treat this as the right side of the fabric. The centre ring is often formed by a number of chains joined together with a slip stitch.

Insert the hook back into the first chain made.

2 Make a slip stitch to join into a ring.

At the beginning of each round one or more chain can be worked to match the height of the following stitches. (This is equivalent to a turning chain).

3 When working trebles three starting chain are required.

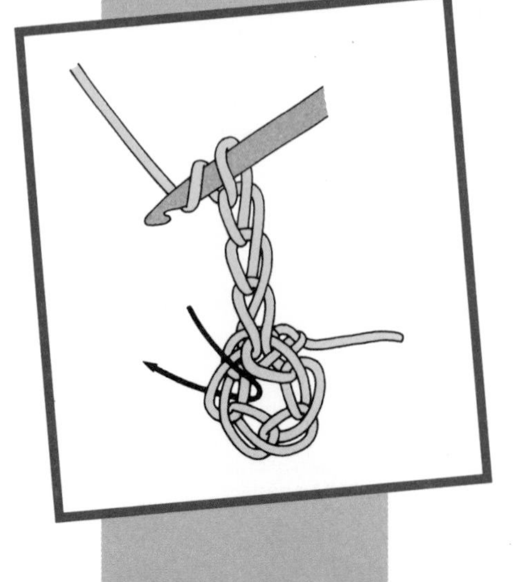

4 The stitches of the first round are worked by inserting the hook into the space at the centre of the chain ring. Occasionally the first round is worked into the first chain (see Motif G on page 22).

5 When each round is complete insert the hook into the top of the chain or stitch at the beginning of the round and slip stitch together.

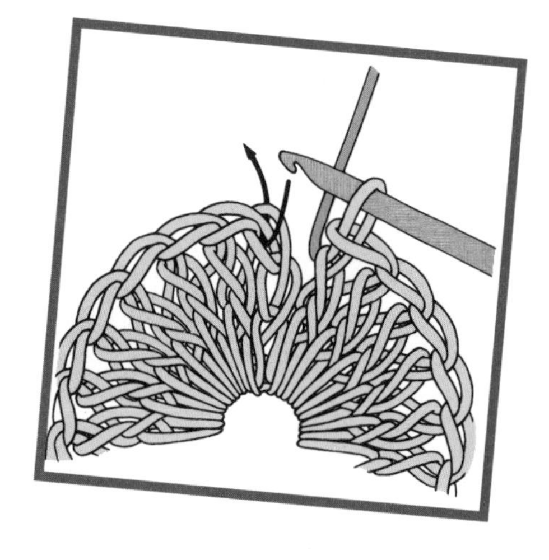

6 When working second and subsequent rounds, unless otherwise stated, insert the hook under the two top loops of the stitches in the previous round.

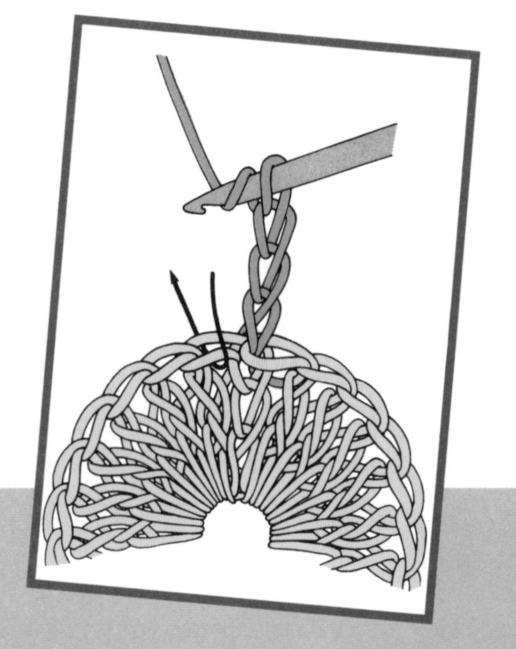

7 After joining final round with a slip stitch, fasten off by making a chain, then cutting the yarn and drawing the end through.

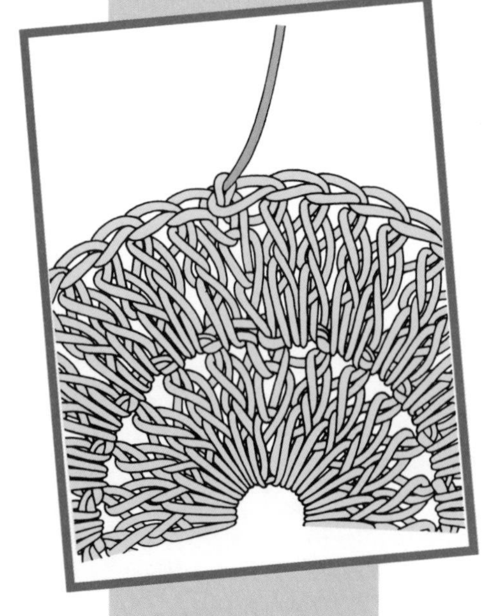

8 Tighten gently to form a knot.

Joining Motifs

The shape of motifs can vary. Some motifs such as triangles, squares and hexagons fit together exactly while others leave interesting spaces when joined. Most motifs can be joined in more than one way so that any individual motif can form the basis of several different fabric designs. If motifs are worked in different colours they can be laid out to produce patchwork effects. Solid motifs are particularly suitable for working coloured patchwork.

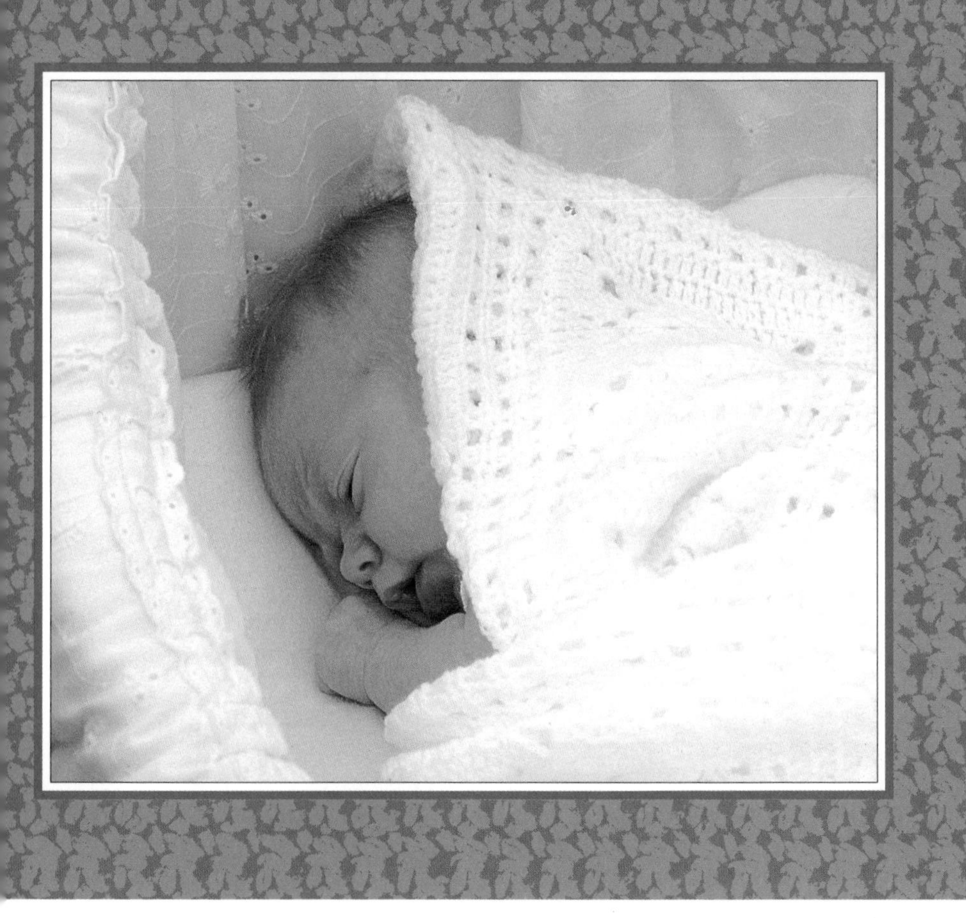

Pattern and Designs

Crochet Shawl

Materials

3 ply: approximately 650 grams.
3.5mm crochet hook.

The quantities of yarn stated are based on average requirements and are therefore approximate.

For notes, abbreviations and how to work from stitch diagrams see pages 43, 44, 45 and 47.

Size

Approximately 142 cm [56 ins] square.

Tension

Motif measures approximately 12.5 x 12.5 cm [5 x 5 ins].

Border and joining pattern: 4 patterns of [2tr, 2ch] = 6 cm [2 1/2 ins], 8 rows = 6 cm [2 1/2 ins].

Motif A (Make 64)

Make 6ch, sl st into first ch to form a ring.

1st round: 3ch (count as 1tr), work 15tr into ring, sl st into 3rd of 3ch at beg of round.

2nd round: 5ch (count as 1tr, 2ch), *work 1tr into next tr, 2ch; rep from * to end, sl st into 3rd of 5ch at beg of round.

3rd round: Sl st into first 2ch sp, 3ch, 2tr into same sp as sl st, 1ch, *work 3tr into next sp, 1ch; rep from * to end, sl st into 3rd of 3ch.

4th round: *[3ch, work 1dc into next ch sp] 3 times, 4ch, 1dc into next ch sp; rep from * 3 times more, sl st into 1st of 3ch at beg of round.

5th round: Sl st into first arch, 3ch, work 2tr into same arch as sl st, 2tr into next arch, 3tr into next arch, work [3tr, 4ch, 3tr] into 4ch arch at corner, *3tr into next arch, 2tr into next arch, 3tr into next arch, [3tr, 4ch, 3tr] into next corner 4ch arch; rep from * twice more, sl st into 3rd of 3ch.

6th round: 3ch, work 1tr into each of next 10tr, [3tr, 1ch, 3tr] into 4ch arch at first corner, *1tr into each of next 14tr, [3tr, 1ch, 3tr] into 4ch arch at next corner; rep from * twice more, 1tr into each of next 3tr, sl st into 3rd of 3ch.

7th round: 3ch, work 1tr into each of next 13tr, [2tr, 1ch, 2tr] into corner ch sp, *1tr into each of next 20tr, [2tr, 1ch, 2tr] into next ch sp; rep from * twice more, 1tr into each of last 6tr, sl st into 3rd of 3ch. Fasten off.

There are 24tr along each side of motif plus 1ch at each corner.

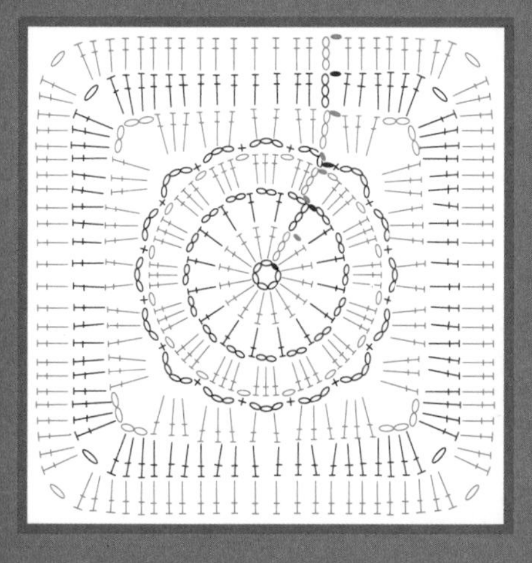

Border and Joining Pattern

Make 294 loose ch.

Foundation row: Work 1dc into 2nd ch from hook, 1dc into next ch, *2ch, miss 1ch, 1dc into each of next 2ch; rep from * to end, turn.

Note: Count each 2ch as **1 st only** throughout.

Commence Pattern

1st row (right side): 3ch (count as 1tr), miss first dc, 1tr into next dc, *2ch, 1tr into each of next 2dc; rep from * to end, turn. 97 patterns of [2tr, 2ch] plus 2tr.

2nd row: 1ch, work 1dc into each of first 2tr, *2ch, 1dc into each of next 2tr; rep from * to end, placing last dc into 3rd of 3ch at beg of previous row, turn.

Rep the last 2 rows 5 times more, then 1st row again.

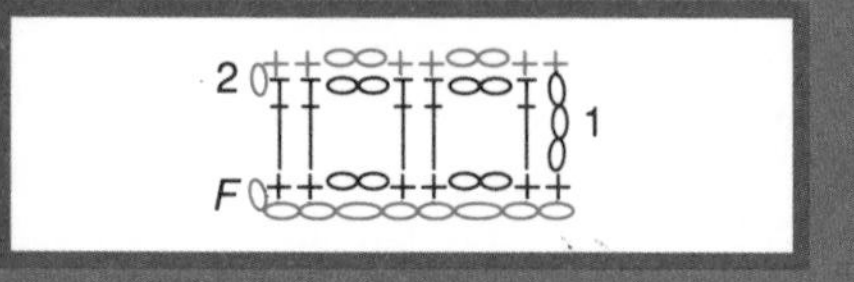

★ **Joining row**: 1ch, work [2dc, 2ch] 6 times, sl st into next tr, **take one of the motifs and, with right sides together, place motif behind border and sl st into ch sp at corner of motif, sl st into next tr on border, *miss 1tr on motif, sl st into next tr, sl st into next tr on border, miss 1tr on motif, sl st into next tr, sl st into ch sp on border , miss 1tr on motif, sl st into next tr, miss 1tr on border, sl st into next tr; rep from * 3 times more, sl st into ch sp at next corner of motif, then sl st back into last tr worked into on border, 2ch, [2dc, 2ch] twice, sl st into next tr; rep from ** until 8 motifs have been joined to form a row, work in pattern to end, turn.

Work Right Side Panel

1st row: 3ch, miss first dc, 1tr into next dc, 2ch, [2tr, 2ch] 5 times (6 patterns worked), miss first tr at side edge of first motif, sl st into next tr, turn.

2nd row:*2ch, 2dc; rep from * to end, turn.

3rd row: Work 6 patterns, miss next 2tr at side of motif, sl st into next tr, turn.

4th row: As 2nd row.

5th row: Work 6 patterns, miss next tr at side of motif, sl st into next tr, turn.

6th row: As 2nd row.

Rep the last 4 rows 3 times more, then 3rd and 4th rows again working sl st into ch sp at corner of motif.

Lengthen remaining loop and drop from hook. Do not break yarn and work from new ball of yarn as follows:

Work Intermediate Joining Panel

With right side facing, rejoin yarn to 2nd tr on remaining side of previous motif and work as follows:

1st row: [2ch, 2tr] twice, 2ch, miss

first tr on side of next motif, sl st into next tr, turn.

2nd row: [2ch, 2dc] twice, 2ch, sl st into same tr as before on previous motif, then sl st into each of next 3tr on motif, turn.

3rd row: [2ch, 2tr] twice, 2ch, miss 2tr on side of next motif, sl st into next tr, turn.

4th row: [2ch, 2dc] twice, 2ch, sl st into same tr as before on previous motif, then sl st into each of next 2tr, turn.

Rep the last 4 rows 3 times more, then 1st and 2nd rows again working sl sts into corner ch sp of each motif. Fasten off.

Work intermediate joining panels between each pair of motifs in the same way.

Work Left Side Panel

With right side facing rejoin yarn to 2nd tr at side edge of last motif and work as follows:

1st row: [2ch, 2tr] 6 times (6 patterns worked), turn.

2nd row: 1ch, [2dc, 2ch] 6 times, sl st into same tr on last motif as before, sl st into each of next 3tr, turn.

3rd row: As 1st row.

4th row: 1ch, [2dc, 2ch] 6 times, sl st into same tr on motif as last sl st, sl st into each of next 2tr, turn.

5th row: As 1st row.

Rep the last 4 rows 3 times more.

18th row: 1ch, [2dc, 2ch] 6 times, sl st into same tr on motif as last sl st, sl st into each of last 2tr and into ch sp at corner, turn.

19th row: As 1st row.

20th row: 1ch, [2dc, 2ch] 6 times, sl st into corner ch sp of motif. Fasten off.

Linking Row

With right side facing pick up dropped loop at edge of right side panel and work as follows:

Work 6 patterns, *1tr into top corner ch sp on next motif, 1tr into first tr, **2ch, miss 1tr on motif, 1tr into each of next 2tr; rep from ** 7 times more placing last tr into 2nd top ch sp, 2ch, [2tr, 2ch] twice across intermediate panel; rep from * 6 times more, then work along last motif as for previous motifs and [2ch, 2tr] 6 times across left side panel ★★.

Work 4 rows in pattern across full width of shawl, thus ending with a right side row ★.

Rep from ★ to ★ 6 times more, then from ★ to ★★ again.

Work 13 rows in pattern across full width of shawl, thus ending with a wrong side row, turn.

Edging

1st round (right side): 1ch, work 2dc into first dc, 1dc into next dc, *1dc into 2ch sp, 1dc into each of next 2dc; rep from * to end working 3dc into last dc. Continue along side edge as follows: *2dc into next pattern, 3dc into next pattern; rep from * to end working 3dc into corner st, work across starting ch as follows: miss first ch, 1dc into next ch, miss 1ch, 1dc into each of next 2ch; rep from * to end working 3dc into last ch, then work along remaining side edge working 5dc into every 2 patterns as for first side edge, 1dc into same st as first 2dc at beg of round, sl st into first dc.

2nd round: 3ch, work 5tr into same dc as last sl st, *miss 2dc, 1dc into next dc, miss 2dc, **7tr into next dc, miss

2dc, 1dc into next dc, miss 2dc; rep from ** to corner dc, work 11tr into corner dc*; rep from * to * 3 times more omitting 6tr at end of last rep, sl st into 3rd of 3ch. Fasten off.

Do not press.

Design Variations

Any of the motifs on the following pages can be used in place of the one worked in the illustrated Shawl. All these motifs have been worked at a basic tension of 20 tr and 11 rows to 10 cm [4 ins] and all have the correct number of stitches on each side to enable you to follow the given instructions for joining.

The Classic Crochet Shawl pattern has 8 rows of 8 motifs with an 8 cm [3 inch] border all round. The Shawl can be varied in size by making more or fewer motifs, and/or working more or fewer pattern repeats in borders and between motifs. Border patterns and stitches between motifs are then calculated as shown in the diagram below.

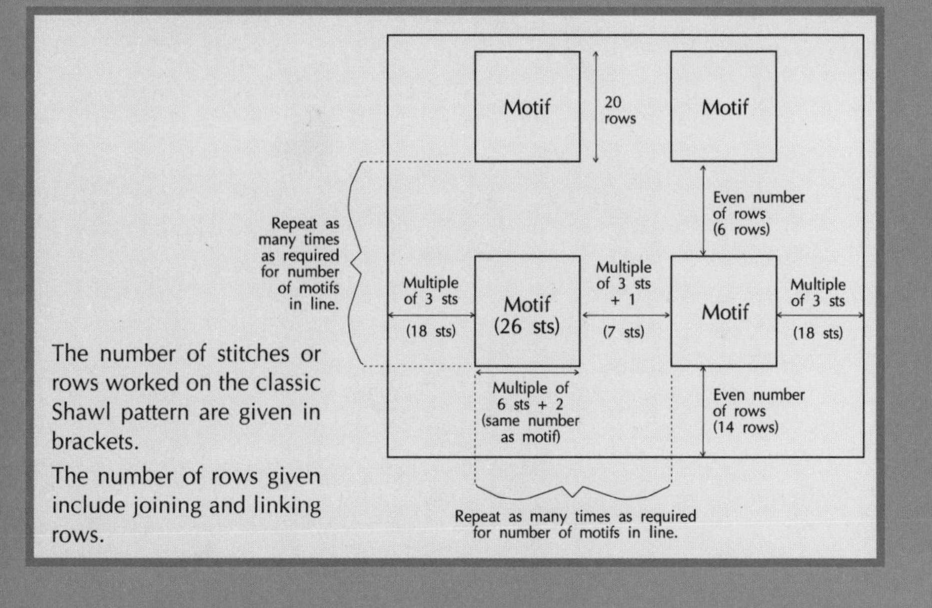

1

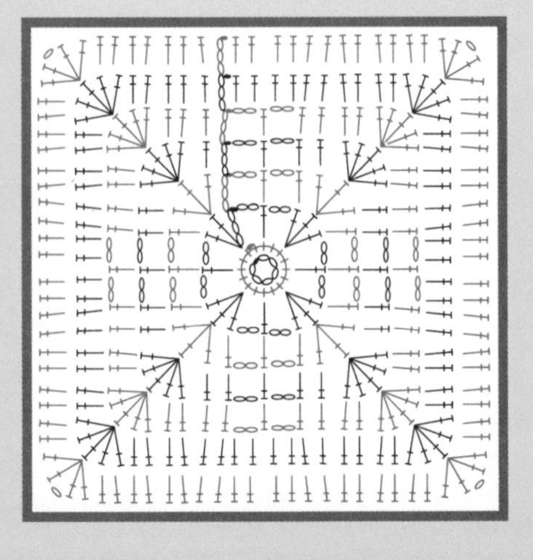

Motif B

Make 6ch, sl st into first ch to form a ring.

1st round: Work 16dc into ring, sl st into first dc.

2nd round: 3ch (count as 1tr), 2tr into same st as last sl st, 2ch, miss 1dc, 1tr into next dc, 2ch, miss 1dc, *3tr into next dc, 2ch, miss 1dc, 1tr into next dc, 2ch, miss 1dc; rep from * twice more, sl st into first dc.

3rd round: 3ch, 3tr into next tr, *1tr into next tr, [2ch, 1tr into next tr] twice, 3tr into next tr; rep from * twice more, [1tr into next tr, 2ch] twice, sl st into 3rd of 3ch at beg of round.

4th round: 3ch, 1tr into next tr, 5tr into next tr, *1tr into each of next 2tr, 2ch, 1tr into next tr, 2ch, 1tr into each of next 2tr, 5tr into next tr; rep from * twice more, 1tr into each of next 2tr, 2ch, 1tr into next tr, 2ch, sl st into 3rd of 3ch at beg of round.

5th round: 3ch, 1tr into each of next 3tr, 5tr into next tr, *1tr into each of next 4tr, 2ch, 1tr into next tr, 2ch, 1tr into each of next 4tr, 5tr into next tr; rep from * twice more, 1tr into each of next 4tr, 2ch, 1tr into next tr, 2ch, sl st into 3rd of 3ch.

6th round: 3ch, 1tr into each of next 5tr, 5tr into next tr, *1tr into each of next 6tr, 2tr into each of next 2 sps, 1tr into each of next 6tr, 5tr into next tr; rep from * twice more, 1tr into each of next 6tr, 2tr into each of next 2 sps, sl st into 3rd of 3ch.

7th round: 3ch, 1tr into each of next 7tr, [2tr, 1ch, 2tr] into next tr, *1tr into each of next 20tr, [2tr, 1ch, 2tr] into next tr; rep from * twice more, 1tr into each of next 12tr, sl st into first dc. Fasten off.

There are 24tr along each side plus 1ch at each corner.

This shawl is worked as the basic pattern but substituting Motif B for the original motif.

2

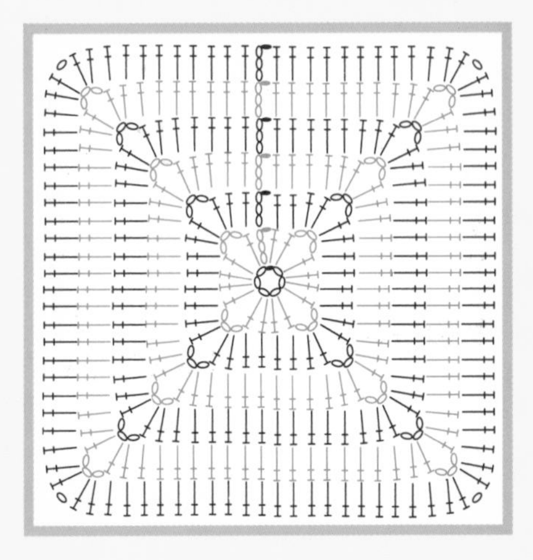

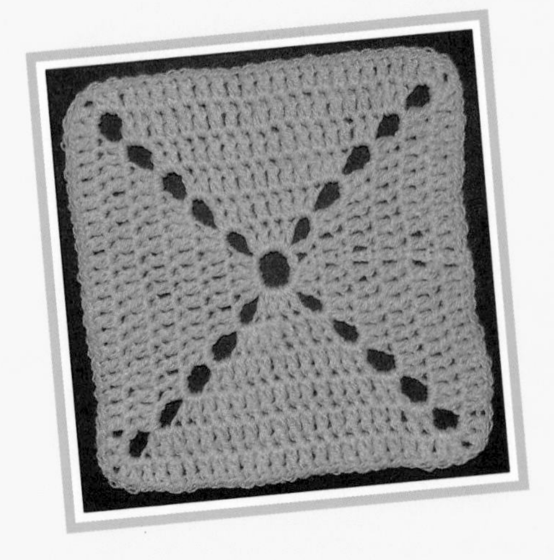

Motif C

Make 6ch, sl st into first ch to form a ring.

1st round: 3ch (count as 1tr), work 1tr into ring, 3ch, [4tr into ring, 3ch] 3 times, 2tr into ring, sl st into 3rd of 3ch at beg of round.

2nd round: 3ch, 1tr into next tr, [2tr, 3ch, 2tr] into 3ch arch, *1tr into each of next 4tr, [2tr, 3ch, 2tr] into next 3ch arch; rep from * twice more, 1tr into each of last 2tr, sl st into 3rd of 3ch.

3rd round: 3ch, 1tr into each of next 3tr, [2tr, 2ch, 2tr] into 3ch arch, *1tr into each of next 8tr, [2tr, 3ch, 2tr] into next 3ch arch; rep from * twice more, 1tr into each of last 4tr, sl st into 3rd of 3ch.

4th round: 3ch, 1tr into each of next 5tr, [2tr, 3ch, 2tr] into 3ch arch, *1tr into each of next 12tr, [2tr, 3ch, 2tr] into next 3ch arch; rep from * twice more, 1tr into each of last 6tr, sl st into 3rd of 3ch.

5th round: 3ch, 1tr into each of next 7tr, [2tr, 3ch, 2tr] into 3ch arch, *1tr into each of next 16tr, [2tr, 3ch, 2tr] into next 3ch arch; rep from * twice more, 1tr into each of last 8tr, sl st into 3rd of 3ch.

6th round: 3ch, 1tr into each of next 9tr, [2tr, 1ch, 2tr] into 3ch arch, *1tr into each of next 20tr, [2tr, 1ch, 2tr] into next 3ch arch; rep from * twice more, sl st into 3rd of 3ch. Fasten off.

There are 24tr at each side edge and 1ch at each corner.

This shawl is worked as the basic shawl but substituting Motif C for the original motif.

3&4

Motif D

Special Abbreviation

Popcorn = work 5tr into next st or space, drop loop from hook, insert hook into top of first tr from front to back, pick up dropped loop and draw through. Work 1ch to secure popcorn.

Make 8ch, sl st into first ch to form a ring.

1st round: 3ch, work 4tr into ring, drop loop from hook, insert hook into top of 3ch, pick up dropped loop and draw through, 1ch to secure (1 popcorn made at beg of round), [5ch, 1 popcorn into ring] 3 times, 5ch, sl st into top of popcorn at beg of round.

2nd round: Sl st into 5ch arch, 3ch (count as 1tr), into same arch as last sl st work [2tr, 2ch, 1 popcorn, 2ch, 3tr], into each of next 3 arches work [3tr, 2ch, 1 popcorn, 2ch, 3tr], sl st into 3rd of 3ch at beg of round.

3rd round: 3ch (count as 1tr), 1tr into each of next 2tr, *2tr into next 2ch sp, 2ch, 1 popcorn into next popcorn, 2ch, 2tr into next 2ch sp, 1tr into each of next 6tr; rep from * 3 times more omitting 3tr at end of last rep, sl st into 3rd of 3ch.

4th round: 3ch, 1tr into each of next 4tr, *2tr into next 2ch sp, 2ch, 1 popcorn, into next popcorn, 2ch, 2tr into next 2ch sp, 1tr into each of next 10tr; rep from * 3 times more omitting 5tr at end of last rep.

5th round: 3ch, 1tr into each of next 6tr, *2tr into next 2ch sp, work [1tr, 3ch, 1tr] into next popcorn, 2tr into next 2ch sp, 1tr into each of next 14tr; rep from * 3 times more omitting 7tr at end of last rep, sl st into 3rd of 3ch.

6th round: 3ch, 1tr into each of next 9tr, *work [2tr, 1ch, 2tr] into next 3ch arch, 1tr into each of next 20tr; rep from * 3 times more omitting 10tr at end of last rep, sl st into 3rd of 3ch. Fasten off.

There are 24tr at each side edge plus 1ch at each corner.

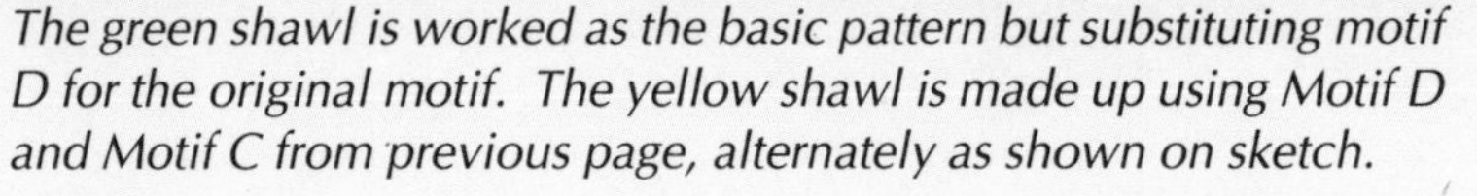

The green shawl is worked as the basic pattern but substituting motif D for the original motif. The yellow shawl is made up using Motif D and Motif C from previous page, alternately as shown on sketch.

5

This shawl is worked as the basic pattern but substituting Motif E for the original motif.

Motif E

Make 6ch, sl st into first ch to form a ring.

1st round: 5ch (count as 1tr, 2ch), *work [1tr, 2ch] 7 times into ring, sl st into 3rd of 5ch at beg of round.

2nd round: Sl st into first sp, 3ch (count as 1tr), 2tr into same sp, *2ch, 3tr into next sp; rep from * to end, 2ch, sl st into 3rd of 3ch at beg of round.

3rd round: 3ch, 1tr into next tr, 3tr into next tr, 2ch, 3tr into next tr, 1tr into each of next 2tr, 2ch, *1tr into each of next 2tr, 3tr into next tr, 2ch, 3tr into next tr, 1tr into each of next 2tr, 2ch; rep from * twice more, sl st into 3rd of 3ch.

4th round: 3ch, 1tr into each of next 3tr, 3tr into next tr, 2ch, 3tr into next tr, 1tr into each of next 4tr, 2ch, *1tr into each of next 4tr, 3tr into next tr, 2ch, 3tr into next tr, 1tr into each of next 4tr, 2ch; rep from * twice more, sl st into 3rd of 3ch.

5th round: 3ch, 1tr into each of next 5tr, 3tr into next tr, 2ch, 3tr into next tr, 1tr into each of next 6tr, 2ch, *1tr into each of next 6tr, 3tr into next tr, 2ch, 3tr into next tr, 1tr into each of next 6tr, 2ch; rep from * twice more, sl st into 3rd of 3ch.

6th round: 3ch, 1tr into each of next 8tr, *work [2tr, 1ch, 2tr] into 2ch sp at corner, 1tr into each of next 9tr, 2tr into next 2ch sp, 1tr into each of next 9tr; rep from * 3 times more omitting 9tr at end of last rep, sl st into 3rd of 3ch. Fasten off.

There are 24tr at each side edge plus 1ch at each corner.

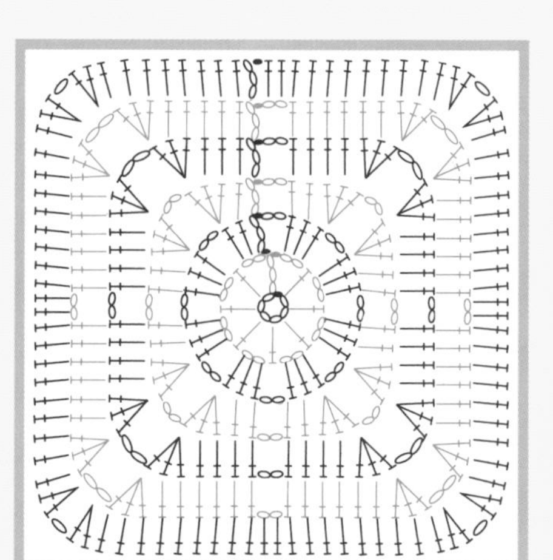

6&7
F F F F F F F F
F F
F F
F F
F F
F F
F F
F F F F F F F F

The pink shawl in the sketch is a smaller version of the classic pattern, using Motif F. 36 (6 x 6) motifs are used, joined as before but with narrower borders (see page 11 for how to work more or less repeats).

Also shown is the layout for a shawl made up mainly with the joining stitch and with 28 motifs around the edge.

Motif F

Special Abbreviation

or **3tr bobble or 4tr bobble =** work 3 (or 4) tr into next st until 1 loop of each remains on hook, yo and through all 4 (or 5) loops on hook.

Make 6ch, sl st into first ch to form a ring.

1st round: 3ch (count as 1tr), work 15tr into ring, sl st into 3rd of 3ch at beg of round.

2nd round: 3ch, 3tr bobble into same st as last sl st, 2ch, 1tr into next tr, 2ch, *4tr bobble into next tr, 2ch, 1tr into next tr, 2ch; rep from * to end, sl st into 3rd of 3ch.

3rd round: Sl st in first sp, 1dc into same sp, *[3ch, 1dc into next sp] 3 times, 5ch, 1dc into next sp; rep from * 3 times more omitting 1dc at end of last rep, sl st into first dc.

4th round: Sl st into first 3ch arch, 3ch, work 2tr into same arch as last sl st until 1 loop of each tr remains on hook, yo and through all 3 loops (3tr bobble made at beg of round), *[2ch, 3tr bobble into next 3ch arch] twice, work [3tr bobble, 3ch, 3tr bobble] into next 5ch arch, 2ch, 3tr bobble into next 3ch arch; rep from * 3 times more, omitting 3tr bobble at end of last rep, sl st into first bobble.

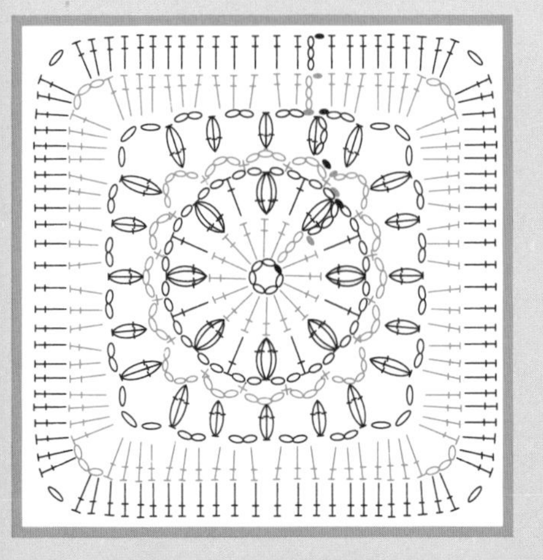

5th round: Sl st into first 2ch sp, 3ch, 2tr into same sp as sl st, *3tr into each of next 2 sps, work [4tr, 3ch, 4tr] into next 3ch arch, 3tr into next sp; rep from * 3 times more, sl st into 3rd of 3ch.

6th round: 3ch, 1tr into each of next 12tr, *work [2tr, 1ch, 2tr] into next 3ch arch, 1tr into each of next 20tr; rep from * 3 times more omitting 13tr at end of last rep, sl st into 3rd of 3ch. Fasten off.

There are 24tr at each side edge plus 1ch at each corner.

8

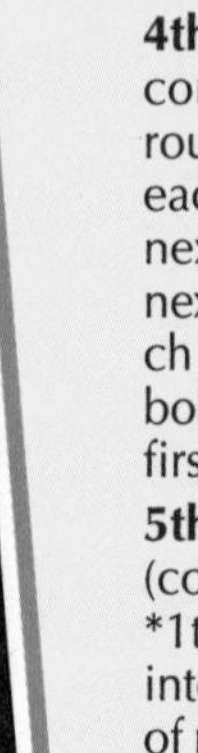

Motif G

Special Abbreviation

3tr bobble or 4tr bobble = work 3 (or 4) tr into next st until 1 loop of each remains on hook, yo and through all 4 (or 5) loops on hook.

1st round: Make 4ch, work 11tr into first of these ch, sl st into 4th of 4ch at beg of round.

2nd round: 3ch, work 2tr into same st as last sl st until 1 loop of each remains on hook, yo and through all 3 loops on hook (3tr bobble made at beg of round), [1ch, 3tr bobble into next tr] twice, 5ch, *3tr bobble into next tr, [1ch, 3tr bobble into next tr] twice, 5ch; rep from * twice more, sl st into top of first bobble.

3rd round: Sl st into first ch sp, 3ch, into same ch sp as last sl st work 3tr until 1 loop of each remains on hook, yo and through all 4 loops on hook (4tr bobble made at beg of round), *1ch, 4tr bobble into next ch sp, 2ch, 5tr into 5ch arch, 2ch, work 4tr bobble into next ch sp; rep from * 3 times more omitting bobble at end of last rep, sl st into top of first bobble.

4th round: Sl st into first ch sp, 3ch then complete first 4tr bobble as on 3rd round, *2ch, 2tr into 2ch sp, 1tr into each of next 2tr, work [1tr, 3ch, 1tr] into next tr, 1tr into each of next 2tr, 2tr into next 2ch sp, 2ch, 4tr bobble into next ch sp; rep from * 3 times more omitting bobble at end of last rep, sl st into top of first bobble.

5th round: Sl st into first 2ch sp, 3ch (count as 1tr), 1tr into same sp as sl st, *1tr into each of next 5tr, 3ch, 4tr bobble into corner 3ch arch, 3ch, 1tr into each of next 5tr, 2tr into each of next 2ch sps; rep from * 3 times more omitting 2tr at end of last rep, sl st into 3rd of 3ch.

6th round: 3ch, 1tr into each of next 6tr, *3tr into next 3ch sp, work [2tr, 1ch, 2tr] into next 4tr bobble, 3tr into next 3ch arch, 1tr into each of next 14tr; rep from * 3 times more omitting 7tr at end of last rep, sl st into 3rd of 3ch. Fasten off.

There are 24tr at each side edge plus 1ch at each corner.

This shawl is worked as the basic pattern but substituting Motif G for the original motif.

9

This shawl is worked as the basic pattern but substituting Motif H for the original motif.

Motif H

Special Abbreviation

Puff st = [yo, insert hook into next st and draw loop through] 4 times into same st (9 loops on hook), yo and through all loops on hook, 1ch to close puff st.

Make 4ch, sl st into first ch to form a ring.

1st round: 3ch (count as 1tr), work 11tr into ring, sl st into 3rd of 3ch at beg of round.

2nd round: 2ch, [yo, insert hook into same st as last sl st and draw yarn through] 3 times (7 loops on hook), yo and through all loops, 1ch to close puff st (1 puff st made at beg of round), [1ch, 1 puff st into next tr] twice, 5ch, *1 puff st into next tr, [1ch, 1 puff st into next tr] twice, 5ch; rep from * twice more, sl st into first puff st.

3rd round: Sl st into first ch sp, 1 puff st into same sp as last sl st, 1ch, 1 puff st into next ch sp, *2ch, 5tr into next 5ch arch, 2ch, 1 puff st into next ch sp, 1ch, 1 puff st into next ch sp; rep from * 3 times more omitting 2 puff sts at end of last rep, sl st into first puff st.

4th round: Sl st into first ch sp, 1 puff st into same sp as last sl st, *2ch, [1tr into next tr, 1ch] twice, work [1tr, 1ch, 1tr, 1ch, 1tr] into next tr, [1ch, 1tr into next tr] twice, 2ch, 1 puff st into next ch sp; rep from * 3 times more omitting 1 puff st at end of last rep, sl st into first puff st.

(1) Miss out this tr. (do 3 ch)
(2) Tr into space only
(3) Do 5 ch

5th round: Sl st into first 2ch sp, 3ch, 1tr into same sp as last sl st, *[1tr into next tr, 1tr into next ch sp] 3 times, 2ch, 1 puff st into next tr, 2ch, [1tr into next ch sp, 1tr into next tr] 3 times, 2tr into each of next 2 2ch sps; rep from * 3 times more omitting 2tr at end of last rep, sl st into 3rd of 3ch.

6th round: 3ch, 1tr into each of next 7tr, *2ch, 1 puff st into next 2ch sp, 3ch, 1 puff st into next 2ch sp, 2ch, 1tr into each of next 16tr; rep from * 3 times more omitting 8tr at end of last rep, sl st into 3rd of 3ch.

7th round: 3ch, work 1tr into each of next 7tr, *2tr into next 2ch sp, work [2tr, 1ch, 2tr] into next 3ch arch, 2tr into next 2ch sp, 1tr into each of next 16tr; rep from * 3 times more omitting 8tr at end of last rep, sl st into 3rd of 3ch. Fasten off.

There are 24tr at each side edge plus 1ch at each corner.

10

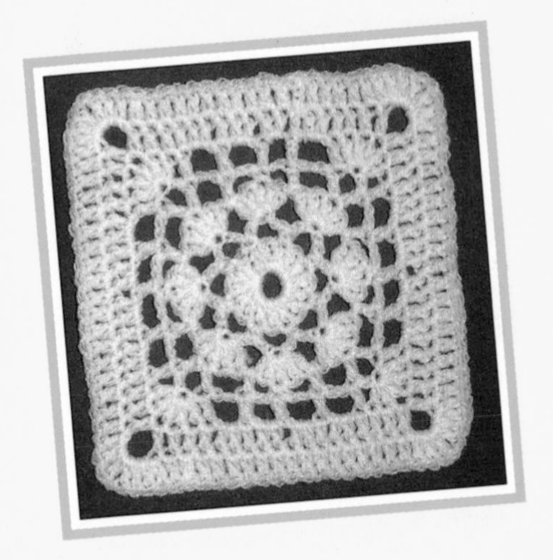

Motif I

Make 6ch, sl st into first ch to form a ring.

1st round: 3ch (count as 1tr), work 15tr into ring, sl st into 3rd of 3ch at beg of round.

2nd round: 1dc into same st as last sl st, [5ch, miss 1tr, 1dc into next tr] 7 times, 2ch, 1tr into first dc.

3rd round: 3ch, work 4tr into top of last tr, [5tr into centre ch of 5ch arch] 7 times, sl st into 3rd of 3ch at beg of round (8 5tr fans worked).

4th round: 5ch (count as 1tr, 2ch), *work [1tr, 3ch, 1tr] into centre tr of next fan, 2ch, 1tr between the 2 fans, 2ch, 1dc into centre tr of next fan, 2ch, 1tr between the 2 fans, 2ch; rep from * 3 times more omitting 1tr and 2ch at end of last rep, sl st into 3rd of 5ch.

5th round: 5ch, 1tr into next tr, work 5tr into next 3ch arch, [1tr into next tr, 2ch] twice, 1tr into next dc, *[2ch, 1tr into next tr] twice, 5tr into next 3ch arch, [1tr into next tr, 2ch] twice, 1tr into next dc; rep from * twice more, 2ch, sl st into 3rd of 5ch.

6th round: 3ch, *2tr into next 2ch sp, 1tr into each of next 3tr, work [1tr, 3ch, 1tr] into next tr, 1tr into each of next 3tr, 2tr into next sp, 1tr into next tr, 2tr into each of next 2 sps, 1tr into next tr; rep from * 3 times more omitting 1tr at end of last rep, sl st into 3rd of 3ch.

7th round: 3ch, 1tr into each of next 6tr, *work [3tr, 1ch, 3tr] into next 3ch arch, 1tr into each of next 18tr; rep from * 3 times more omitting 7tr at end of last rep, sl st into 3rd of 3ch. Fasten off.

There are 24tr at each side edge plus 1ch at each corner.

For a two colour motif work the first three rounds in colour A and the remaining four rounds in colour B.

The shawl shown consists of Motif I in one colour and two colours as given above. Place coloured motifs as shown in the sketch, or plan your own design.

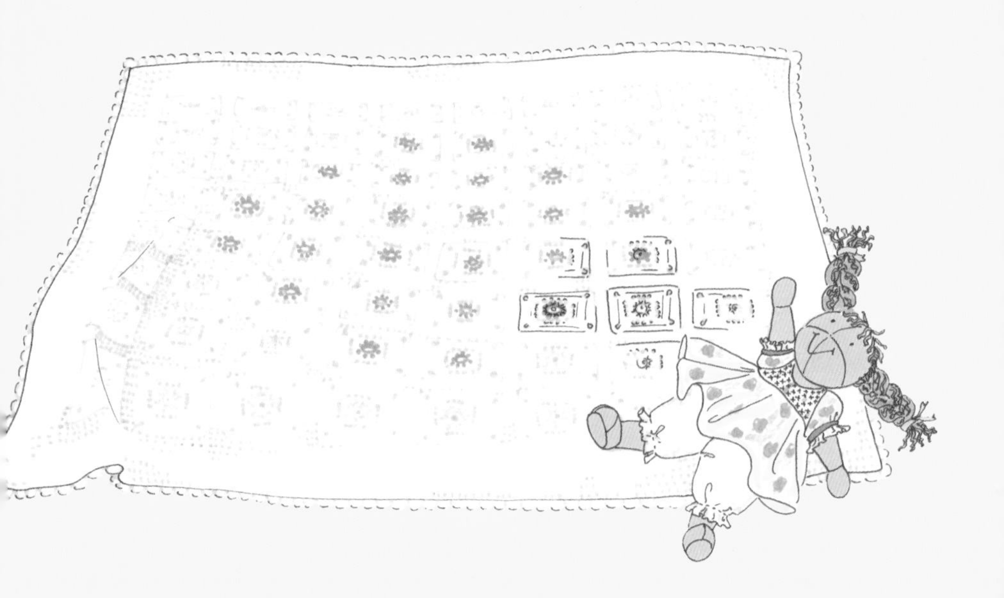

11 & 12

A	B	C	D	E	F	G	H
B	C	D	E	F	G	H	I
C	D	E	F	G	H	I	J
D	E	F	G	H	I	J	A
E	F	G	H	I	J	A	B
F	G	H	I	J	A	B	C
G	H	I	J	A	B	C	D
H	I	J	A	B	C	D	E

Motif J

Special Abbreviation

Puff st = *yo, insert hook into next st, yo and draw loop through; rep from * 4 times more into same st as before, yo and through all loops on hook, 1ch to secure.

Make 8ch, sl st into first ch to form a ring.

1st round: 2ch, *yo, insert hook into ring, yo and draw loop through; rep from * 3 times more, yo and through all loops on hook, 1ch to secure (1 puff st made at beg of round), 2ch, work [1 puff st, 2ch] 7 times into ring, sl st into first puff st.

2nd round: 5ch (count as 1tr and 2ch), 1tr into same puff st, *2ch, [puff st into next sp, 2ch] twice**, work a V st of [1tr, 2ch, 1tr] into next puff st; rep from * twice and from * to ** again, sl st into 3rd of 5ch.

3rd round: Sl st into next ch, 5ch (count as 1tr and 2ch), 1tr into same sp, *2ch, [1 puff st into next sp, 2ch] 3 times**, V st into next sp at corner; rep from * twice and from * to ** again, sl st into 3rd of 5ch.

4th round: As for 3rd round but work 4 puff sts along each side of square.

5th round: As for 3rd round but work 5 puff sts along each side of square.

6th round: 2ch (count as 1htr), *work [2htr, 2ch, 2htr] into corner sp, 1htr into next tr, [2htr into next sp, 1htr into next puff st] twice, 2htr into each of next 2 sps, [1htr into next puff st, 2htr into next sp] twice, 1htr into next tr; rep from * 3 times more omitting 1htr at end of last rep, sl st into 2nd of 2ch.

7th round: 2ch, 1htr into each of next 2htr, *work [1htr, 1ch, 1htr] into corner sp, 1htr into each of next 22htr; rep from * 3 times more omitting 3tr at end of last rep, sl st into 2nd of 2ch. Fasten off.

There are 24htr along each side plus 1ch at each corner. When joining this square treat each htr as a tr.

The sketch shows a shawl worked as the basic pattern but substituting Motif J for the original motif. Also shown is a layout for a shawl with all the different motifs used in place of the one original motif.

Crochet Know How

In the following pages we have given step by step instructions and diagrams on how to work the basic crochet stitches, understand crochet diagrams and work from pattern instructions.

Equipment

Crochet Hooks

Crochet hooks are usually made from steel, aluminium or plastic in a range of sizes according to their diameter. As each crochet stitch is worked separately until only one loop remains on the hook, space is not needed to hold stitches and the hooks are made to a standard convenient length.

Holding the Hook and Yarn

There are no hard and fast rules as to the best way to hold the hook and yarn. The diagrams below show just one method, but choose whichever way you find the most comfortable.

Due to the restrictions of space it is not possible to show diagrams for both right and left handed people. Left handers may find it easier to trace the diagrams and then turn the tracing paper over, thus reversing the image, alternatively reflect the diagrams in a mirror. Read left for right and right for left where applicable.

The hook is held in the right hand as if holding a pencil.

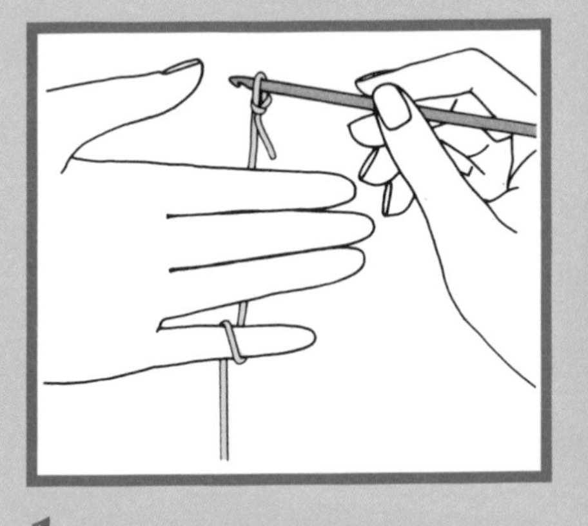

1 To maintain the slight tension in the yarn necessary for easy, even working, it can help to arrange the yarn around the fingers of the left hand in this way.

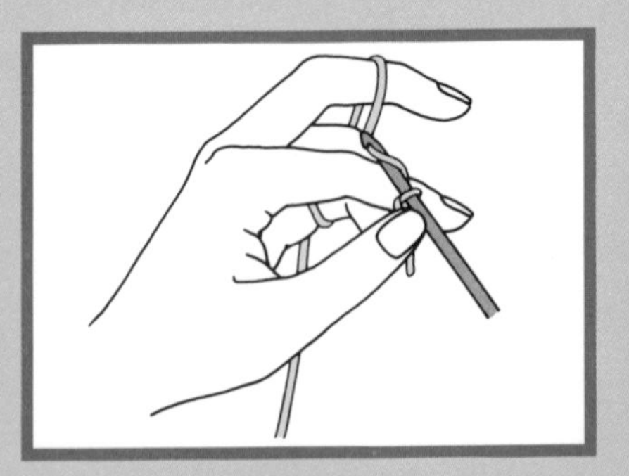

2 The left hand holds the work and at the same time controls the yarn supply. The left hand middle finger is used to manipulate the yarn, while the index finger and thumb hold on to the work.

To Start

Almost all crochet begins with a base or starting chain, which is a series of chain stitches, beginning with a slip knot.

Slip Knot

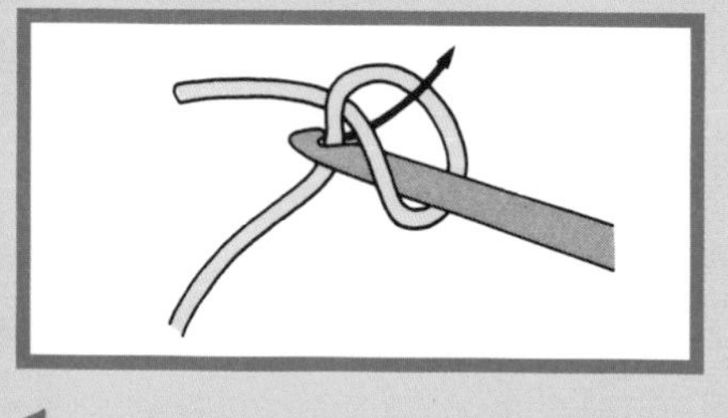

1 Make a loop then hook another loop through it.

2 Tighten gently and slide the knot up to the hook.

Yarn Over (yo)

Wrap the yarn from back to front over the hook (or hold the yarn still and manoeuvre the hook). This movement of the yarn over the hook is used over and over again in crochet and is usually called 'yarn over', abbreviated as 'yo'.

Chain Stitch (ch ○)

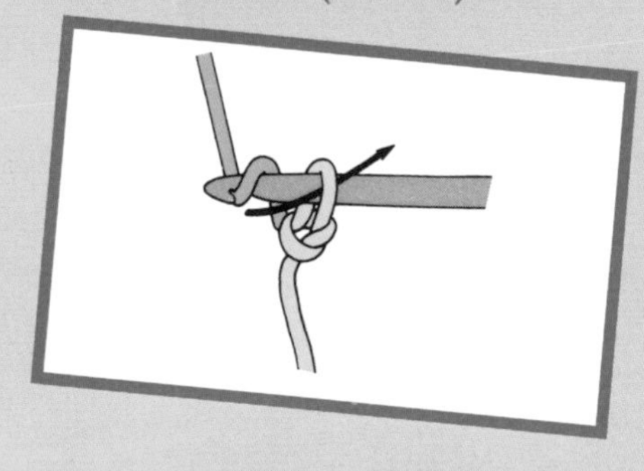

Yarn over and draw through the loop on the hook to form a new loop without tightening up the previous one.

Repeat to form as many chains as required. Do not count the slip knot as a stitch.

Note: Unless otherwise stated, when working into the starting chain always work under two strands of chain loops as shown in the diagrams.

Basic Stitches

Crochet patterns are usually produced using combinations of the following basic stitches. We have shown them worked into a starting chain but the method is the same wherever the stitch is used.

Slip Stitch (sl st ●)

This is the shortest of crochet stitches and unlike other stitches is not used on its own to produce a fabric. It is used for joining, shaping and where necessary carrying the yarn to another part of the fabric for the next stage.

1 Insert the hook into the work (second chain from hook on starting chain), yarn over and draw the yarn through both the work and loop on the hook in one movement.

2 To join a chain ring with a slip stitch, insert hook into first chain, yarn over and draw through the work and the loop on the hook.

Double Crochet (dc +)

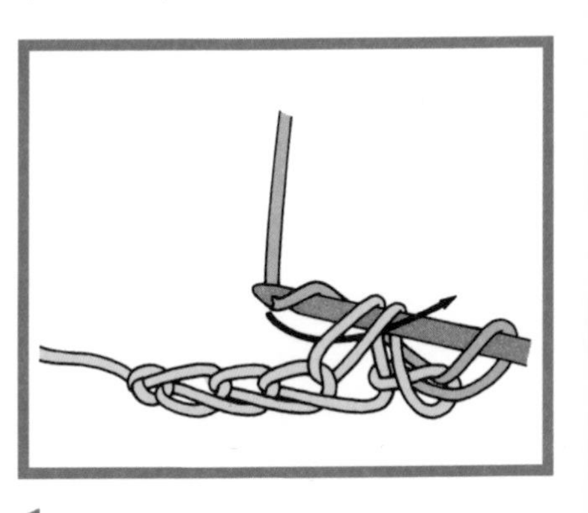

1 Insert the hook into the work (second chain from hook on starting chain), *yarn over and draw yarn through the work only.

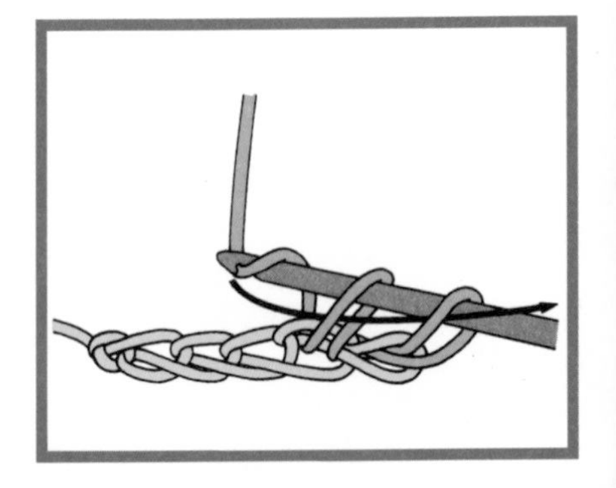

2 Yarn over again and draw the yarn through both loops on the hook.

3 1 dc made. Insert hook into next stitch; repeat from * in step 1.

Half Treble (htr 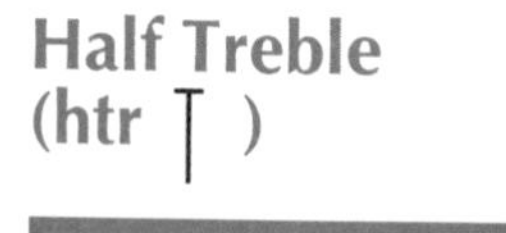)

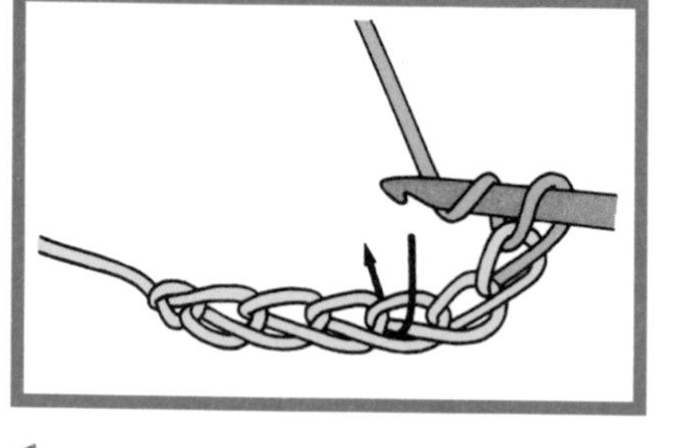

1 Yarn over and insert the hook into the work (third chain from hook on starting chain).

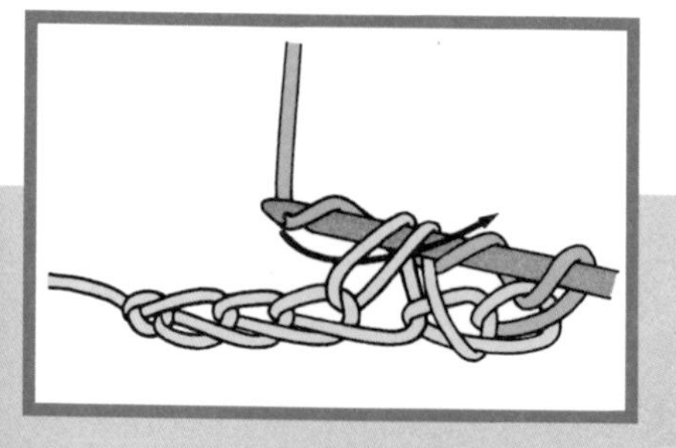

2 *Yarn over and draw through the work only.

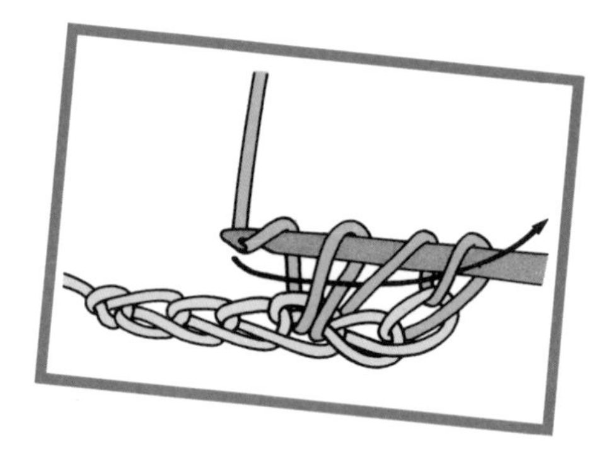

3 Yarn over again and draw through all three loops on the hook.

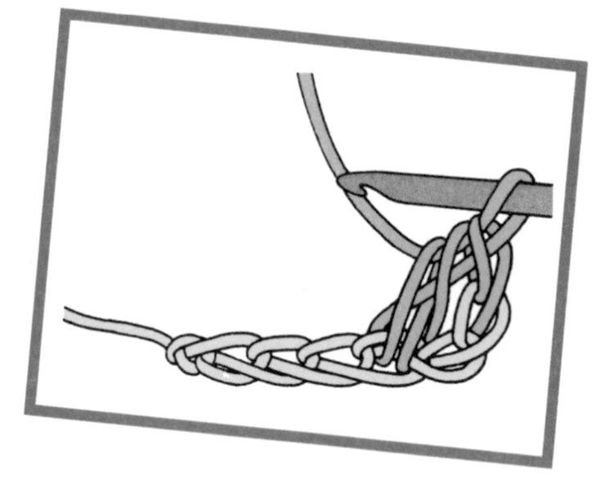

4 1 htr made. Yarn over, insert hook into next stitch; repeat from * in step 2.

Treble (tr ⫪)

1 Yarn over and insert the hook into the work (fourth chain from hook on starting chain).

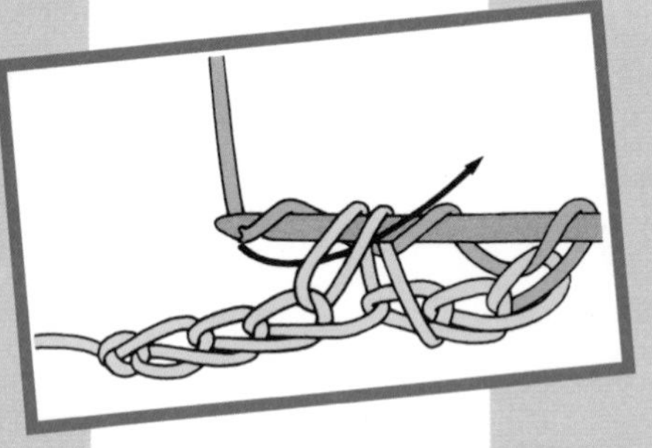

2 *Yarn over and draw through the work only.

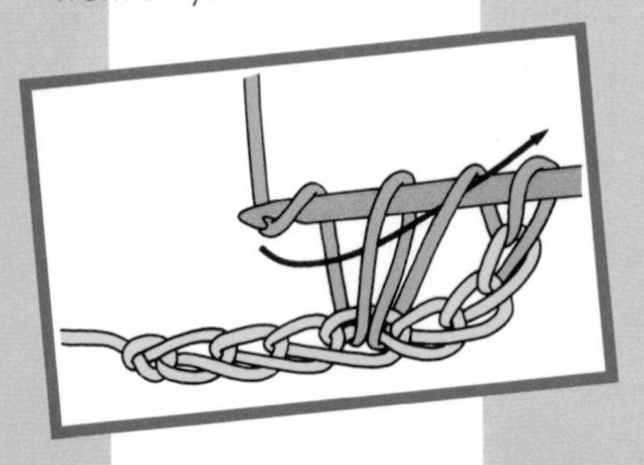

3 Yarn over and draw through the first two loops only.

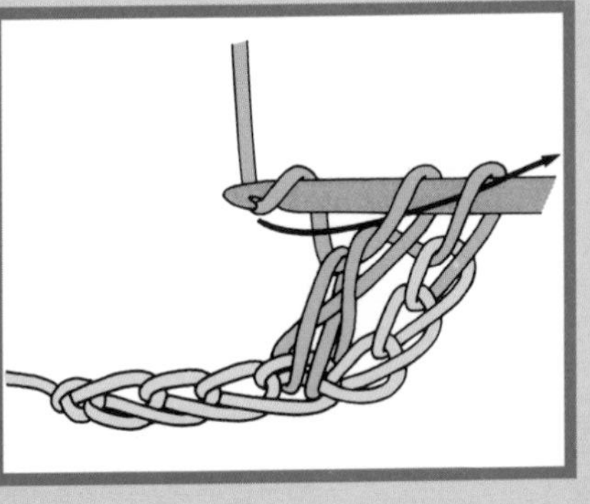

4 Yarn over and draw through the last two loops on the hook.

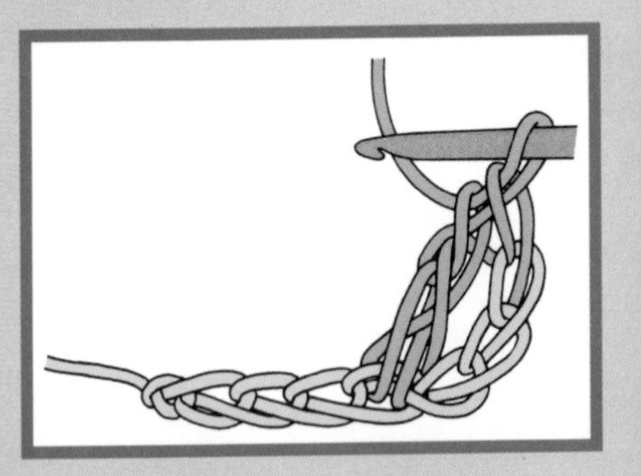

5 1 tr made. Yarn over, insert hook into next stitch; repeat from * in step 2.

Double Treble

(dtr ⫲)

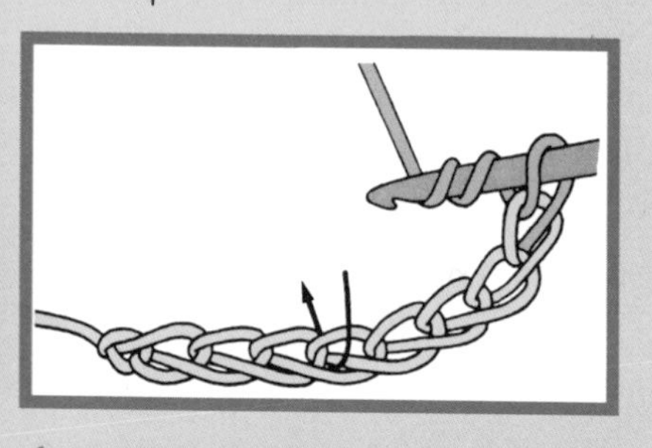

1 Yarn over twice, insert the hook into the work (fifth chain from hook on starting chain).

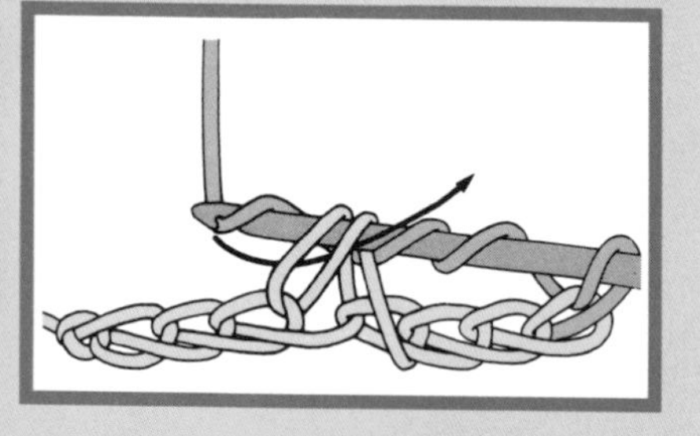

2 *Yarn over and draw through the work only.

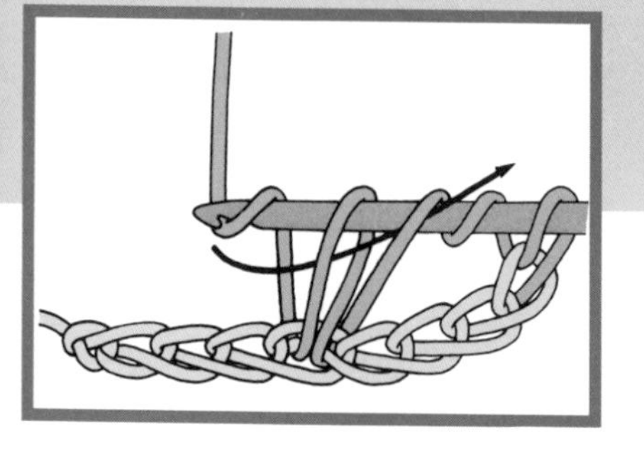

3 Yarn over again and draw through the first two loops only.

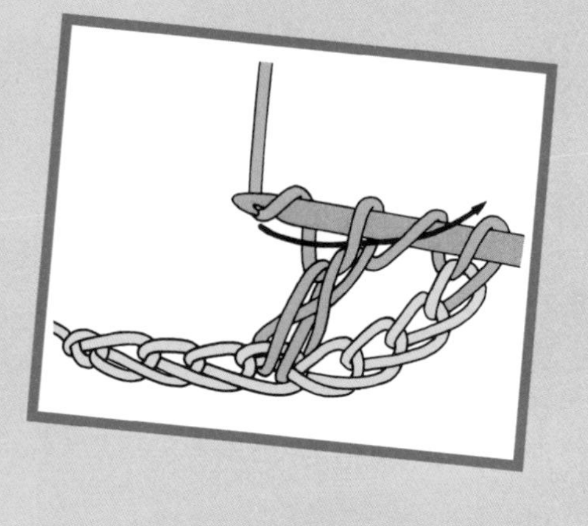

4 Yarn over again and draw through the next two loops only.

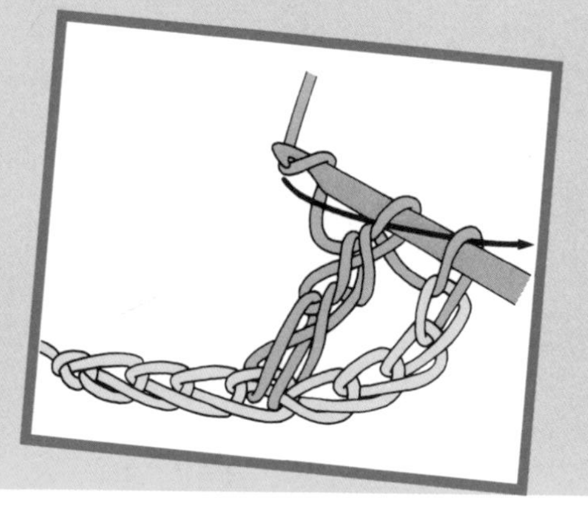

5 Yarn over again and draw through the last two loops on the hook.

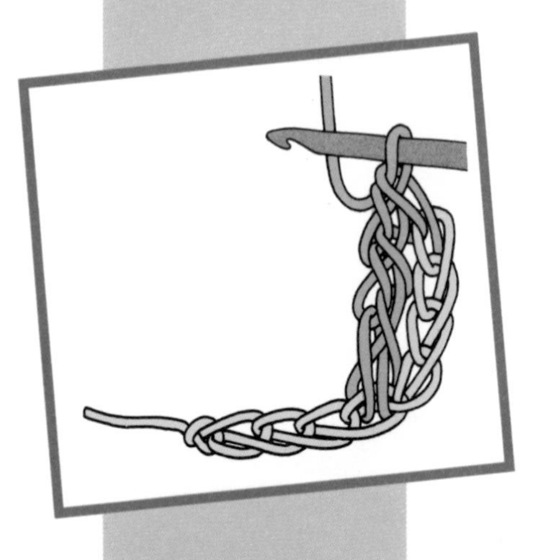

6 1 dtr made. Yarn over twice, insert hook into next stitch; repeat from * in step 2.

Longer Basic Stitches

Triple treble (ttr), quadruple treble (quadtr), quintuple treble (quintr) etc. are made by wrapping the yarn over three, four, five times etc. at the beginning and finishing as for a double treble, repeating step 4 until two loops remain on hook, finish with step 5.

Making Crochet Fabric

These are the basic procedures for making crochet fabrics.

Starting Chain

To make a flat fabric worked in rows you must begin with a starting chain. The length of the starting chain is the number of stitches needed for the first row of fabric plus the number of chain needed to get to the correct height of the stitches to be used in the first row.

Working in Rows

A flat fabric can be produced by turning the work at the end of each row. Right handers work from right to left and left handers from left to right. One or more chain must be worked at the beginning of each row to bring the hook up to the height of the first stitch in the row. The number of chain used for turning depends upon the height of the stitch they are to match as follows:

double crochet = 1 chain

half treble = 2 chain

treble = 3 chain

double treble = 4 chain

When working half trebles or longer stitches the turning chain takes the place of the first stitch. Where one chain is worked at the beginning of a row starting with double crochet it is usually for height only and is in addition to the first stitch.

Basic Treble Fabric

Make a starting chain of the required length plus two chain. Work one

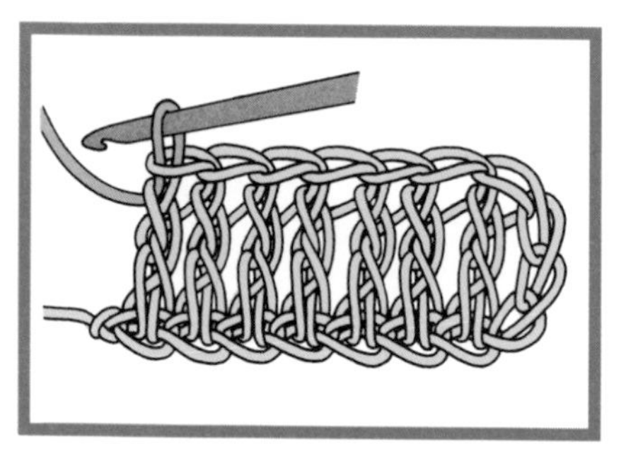

treble into fourth chain from hook. The three chain at the beginning of the row form the first treble. Work one treble into the next and every chain to the end of the row.

At the end of each row turn the work so that another row can be worked across the top of the previous one. It does not matter which way the work is turned but be consistent. Make three chain for turning. These turning chain will count as the first treble.

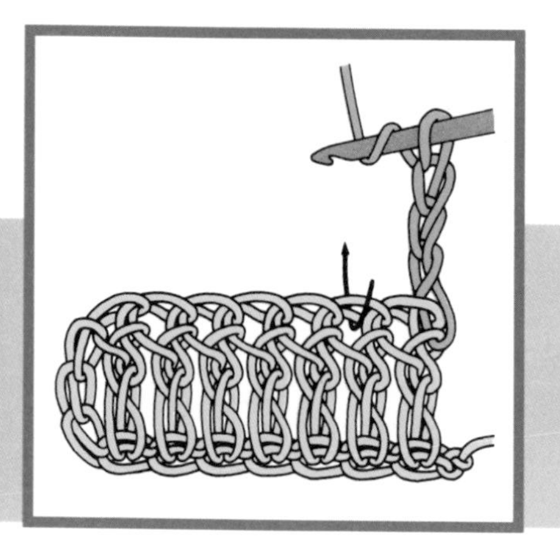

Miss the first treble in the previous row, work a treble into the top of the next and every treble including the last treble in row, then work a treble into third of three chain at the beginning of the previous row.

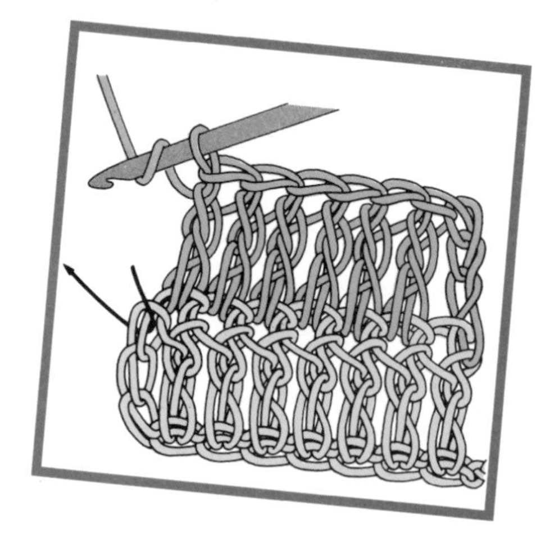

Note: Unless otherwise stated when working into the top of a stitch, always work under two strands as shown in diagrams.

Fastening Off

To fasten off the yarn permanently break off the yarn about 5cm [2 ins] away from the work (longer if you need to sew pieces together). Draw the end through the loop on hook and tighten gently.

Joining in New Yarn and Changing Colour

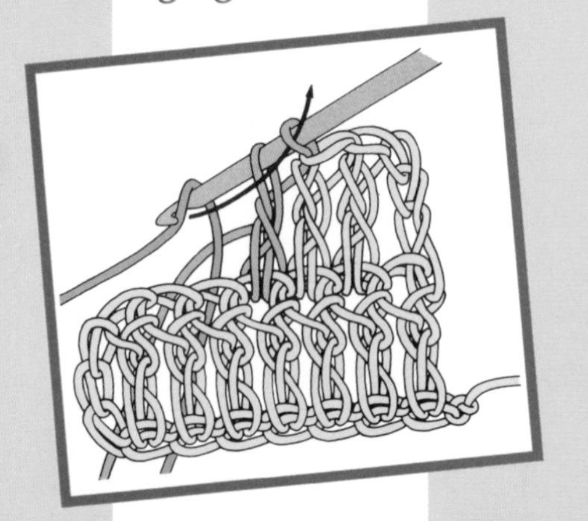

When joining in new yarn or changing colour, work in the old yarn until two loops of the last stitch remain in the old yarn or colour. Use the new colour or yarn to complete the stitch.

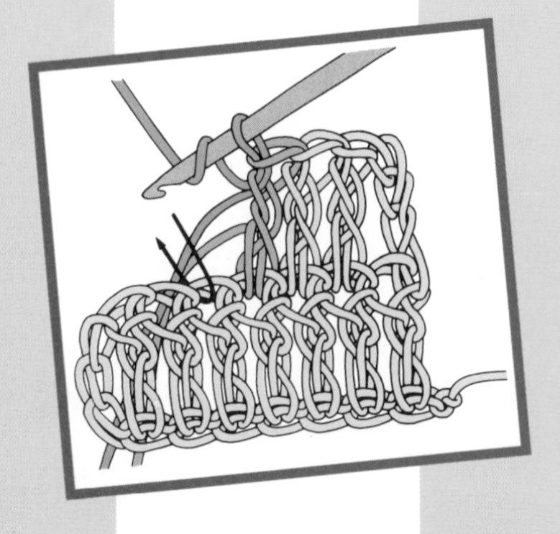

Continue to work the following stitches in the new colour or yarn, as before.

If you are working whole rows in different colours, make the change during the last stitch in the previous row, so the new colour for the next row is ready to work the turning chain.

Do not cut off any yarns which will be needed again later at the same edge, but continue to use them as required, leaving an unbroken 'float' thread up the side of the fabric.

If, at the end of a row, the pattern requires you to return to the beginning of the same row without turning and to work another row in a different colour in the same direction, complete the first row in the old colour and fasten off by lengthening the final loop on the hook, passing the whole ball through it and gently tighten again. That yarn is now available if you need to rejoin it later at this edge (if not, cut it).

Stitch Variations

Most crochet stitch patterns, however elaborate, are made using combinations of basic stitches. Different effects can be created by small variations in the stitch making procedure or by varying the position and manner of inserting the hook into the fabric. The following techniques are used frequently to build up crochet fabric.

Note: Terms such as 'group', 'cluster', 'picot', 'shell', 'fan', 'flower', 'petal', 'leaf' and 'bobble' do not denote a fixed arrangement of stitches. Exactly what they mean may be different for each pattern and this would usually be given at the beginning of each set of instructions as a Special Abbreviation.

Groups or Shells

These consist of several complete stitches worked into the same place. They can be worked as part of a pattern or as a method of increasing.

Five Treble Group

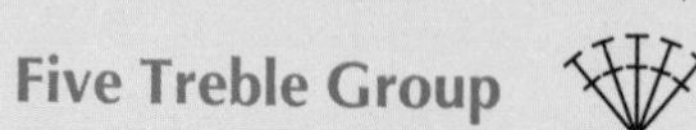

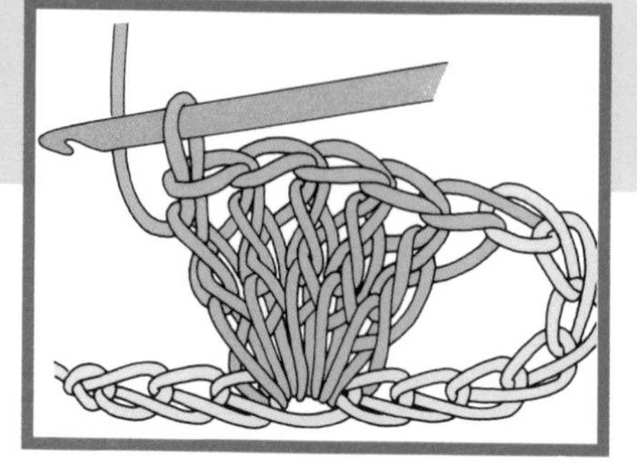

Work five trebles into one stitch.

Groups and shells can be worked in half trebles, trebles and double trebles, and on diagrams the point at the base of the group will be positioned above the space or stitch where the hook is to be inserted.

Clusters

Any combination of stitches may be joined into a cluster by leaving the last loop of each temporarily on the hook until they are worked off together at the end. Working stitches together in this way can also be a method of decreasing.

It is important to be sure exactly how and where the hook is to be inserted for each 'leg' of the cluster. The 'legs' may be worked over adjacent stitches, or stitches may be missed between 'legs'.

Three Treble Cluster

(Worked over adjacent stitches).

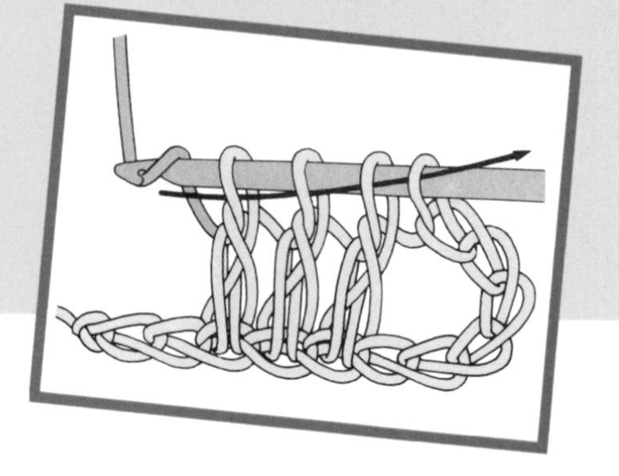

1 Work a treble into each of the next three stitches leaving the last loop of each treble on the hook.

2 Yarn over and draw through all four loops on the hook.

Clusters can be worked in half trebles, trebles, double trebles or longer stitches, on the diagrams each 'leg' of the cluster will be positioned above the stitch where the hook is to be inserted.

Bobbles

When a cluster is worked into one stitch it forms a bobble.

Five Treble Bobble 

1 Work five trebles into one stitch leaving the last loop of each on the hook.

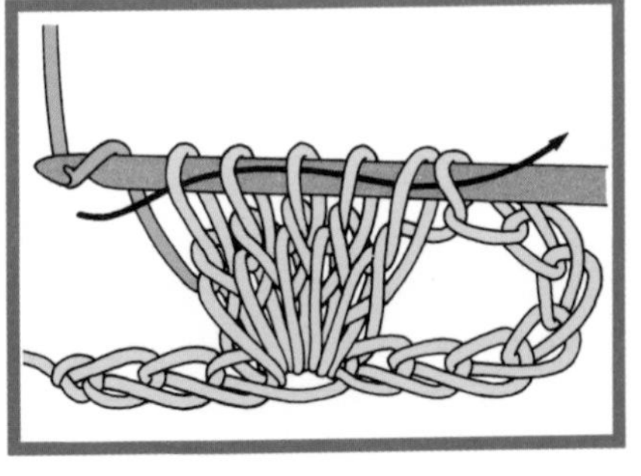

2 Yarn over and draw through all the loops on the hook.

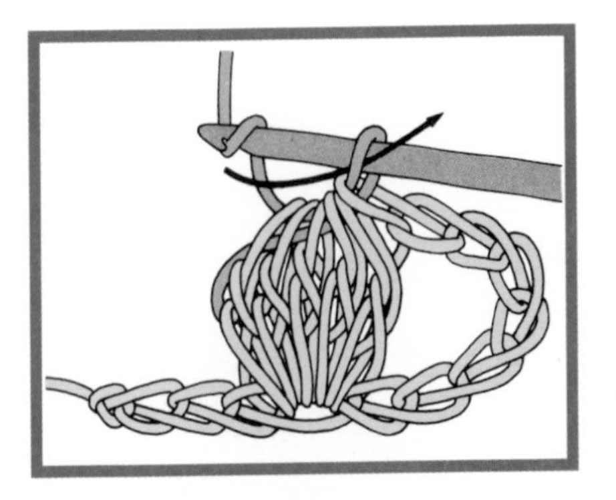

More bulky bobbles can be secured with an extra chain stitch.

Bobbles can be worked in half trebles, trebles, double trebles or longer stitches, on the diagrams they are postioned above the stitch or space where the hook is to be inserted.

Popcorns

Popcorns are groups of complete stitches usually worked into the same place, folded and closed at the top. An extra chain can be worked to secure the popcorn.

Five Treble Popcorn

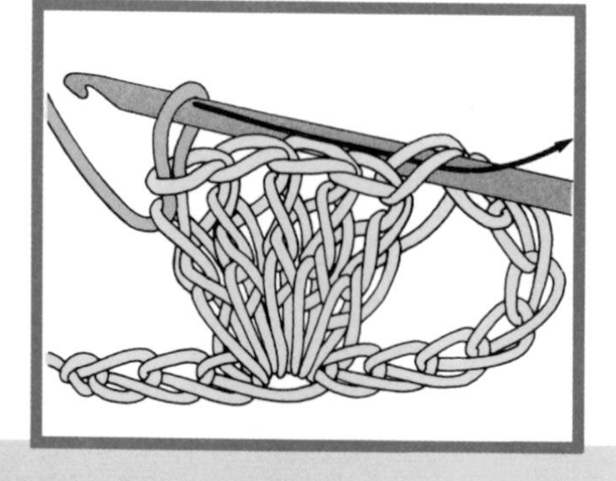

1 Work five trebles into one stitch. Take the hook out of the working loop and insert it into the top of the first treble made from front to back.

2 Pick up the working loop and draw this through to close the popcorn. If required work one chain to secure the popcorn.

Popcorns can be worked in half trebles, trebles, double trebles or longer stitches, on the diagrams the point at the base of the popcorn will be positioned above the space or stitch where it is to be worked.

Puff Stitches

These are similar to bobbles but worked using half trebles, into the same stitch or space. However because half trebles cannot be worked until one loop remains on the hook, the stitches are not closed until the required number have been worked.

Three Half Treble Puff Stitch

(Worked into one stitch).

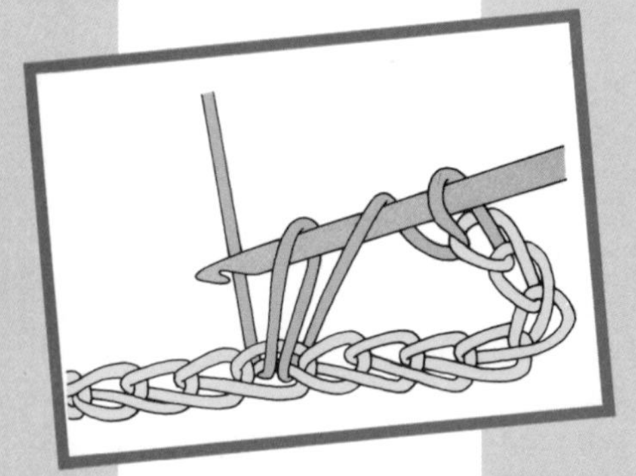

1 Yarn over, insert the hook, yarn over again and draw a loop through (three loops on the hook).

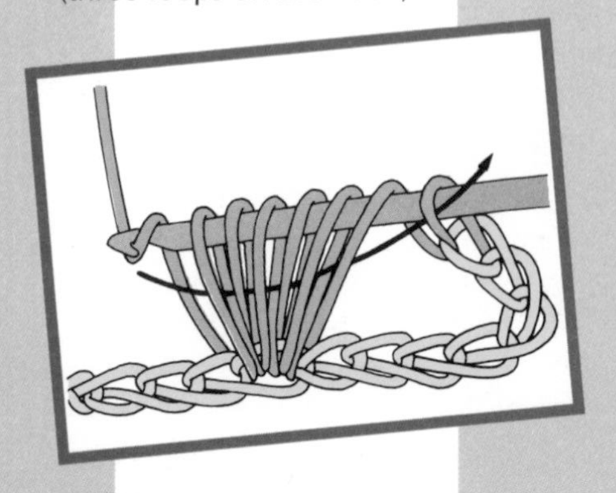

2 Repeat this step twice more, inserting the hook into the same stitch (seven loops on the hook); yarn over and draw through all the loops on the hook.

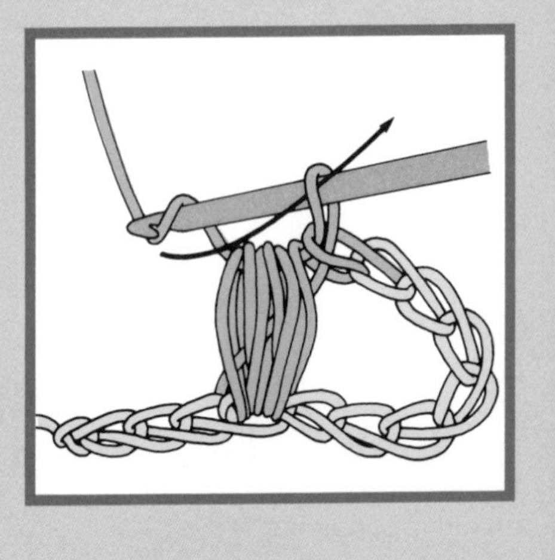

3 As with popcorns and bulky bobbles an extra chain stitch is often used to secure the puff stitch firmly. This will be indicated within the pattern if necessary.

A **cluster** of half treble stitches is worked in the same way as a puff stitch but each 'leg' is worked where indicated.

Picots

A picot is normally a chain loop formed into a closed ring by a slip stitch or double crochet. The number of chains in a picot can vary.

Four Chain Picot

(Closed with a slip stitch).

1 Work four chain.

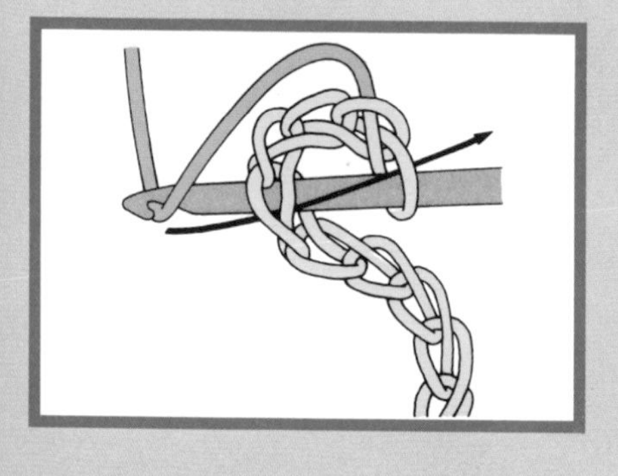

2 Into fourth chain from hook work a slip stitch to close.

3 Continue working chain or required stitch.

Note: When working a picot closed with a slip stitch at the top of a chain arch, the picot will not appear central unless an extra chain is worked after the slip stitch.

Pattern Instructions

In order to follow crochet instructions you should know how to make the basic stitches and be familiar with basic fabric-making procedures.

Any unusual stitches or combinations of stitches are usually given as a Special Abbreviation with the particular pattern.

All the patterns in this book have been given in the form of both written instructions and diagrams, so that you can choose to follow either method.

However, if you are more used to written instructions it is still a good idea to look at the diagram to get an overall picture of how the design has been put together.

Diagram followers may find it helpful to refer to the written instructions to confirm their interpretation of the diagram.

Working from a Diagram

Diagrams should be read exactly as the crochet is worked. For example, motifs are worked from the centre outwards and all-over patterns from the bottom to the top. Each stitch is represented by a symbol that has been drawn to resemble its crocheted equivalent. The position of the symbol shows where the stitch should be worked.

Stitch symbols are drawn and laid out as realistically as possible but there are times when they have to be distorted for the sake of clarity. For example stitches may look extra long to show clearly where they are to be placed, but you should not try to make artificially long stitches. This distortion is particularly apparent on diagrams that represent fabrics not intended to lie flat.

Right Side and Wrong Side Rows

Where the work is turned after each row only alternate rows are worked with the right side of the work facing.

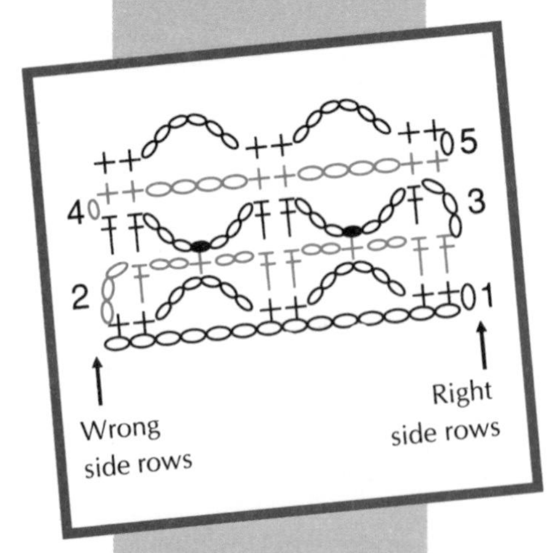

These 'right side rows' are printed in black on stitch diagrams and read from right to left. Wrong side rows are printed in blue and read from left to right. Row numbers are shown at the side of the diagrams at the **beginning** of the row.

Patterns worked in rounds have the right side facing on every round. To make them easier to follow we have printed alternate rounds in black and blue.

Starting Chains and Pattern Repeats

The number of starting chain required is given with each pattern. It may be given in the form of a multiple, for example:- **Starting chain: Multiple of 7 sts + 3.** This means you can make any length of chain that is a multiple of 7 + 3, such as 14 + 3ch, 21 + 3ch, 28 + 3ch etc.

In the written instructions the stitches that should be repeated are contained within brackets [ ] or follow an asterisk *. These stitches are repeated across the row or round the required number of times. On the diagrams the stitches that have to be repeated can be easily visualised. The extra stitches not included in the pattern repeat are there to balance the row or make it symmetrical and are only worked once. Obviously turning chains are only worked at the beginning of each row. Some diagrams consist of more than one pattern repeat so that you can see more clearly how the design is worked.

Tension (or Gauge)

This refers to the number of stitches and rows in a given area. When following a pattern for a garment or other article the instructions will include a specified tension. If you do not produce fabric with the same number of stitches and rows as indicated, your work will not come to the measurements given.

To ensure that you achieve the correct tension work a tension sample or swatch before starting the main part of the crochet. The hook size quoted in the pattern is a suggestion only. You must use whichever hook gives you the correct tension.

It is worth experimenting with different hook sizes so that you find the best tension for your chosen pattern and yarn. Some stitches look and feel better worked loosely and others need to be worked more firmly to be at their best.

Pressing and Finishing

The methods you use to finish your crochet depend largely on what you are using it for and what yarn you have used.

Cotton

Cotton yarns benefit from being wetted or thoroughly steamed. If you are using household starch (as opposed to spray starch) now is the time to apply it, either by immersing the crocheted piece or dabbing the wet starch on to the material. Pin out very near to the edge, at very close intervals, stretching or easing the material to ensure that it is even. Picots, bobbles or other intrinsic features should be carefully placed with a pin at this stage. Having satisfied yourself that the shape is correct, the work can now be pressed using a hot iron. Do not allow the full weight of the iron to rest on the work especially where interesting textures are involved. Remove the pins and if required make fine adjustments to the edges of the material to ensure that they are straight. Now leave until the work is **thoroughly** dry.

Motifs

Work as given above but leave the pins in position until the work is **thoroughly** dry. Ensure that all three-dimensional features show to their best advantage.

Other Yarns

In principal the methods given for working with cotton yarns apply, but you must read the finishing or pressing information usually included with your yarn. Not every yarn will be suitable for or require starching and some yarns cannot be pressed with a hot iron.

Joining Seams

Various methods can be used to join pieces of crochet. The use of the item will often dictate the method used, the seam could be invisible or decorative. Below are a few suggestions for joining pieces of crochet.

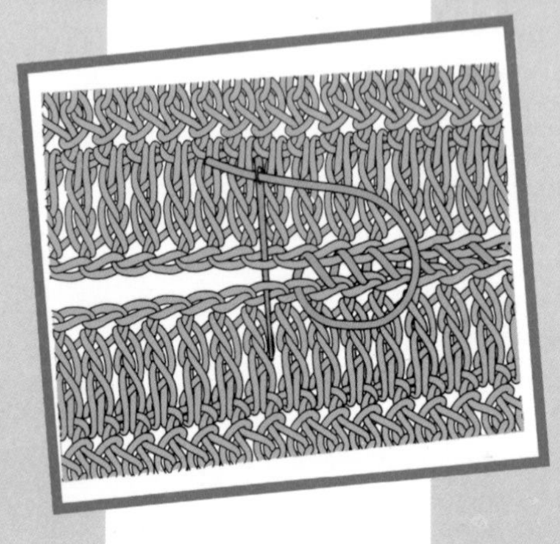

To join with an invisible sewn seam, place pieces edge to edge with the wrong sides uppermost and whip stitch together.

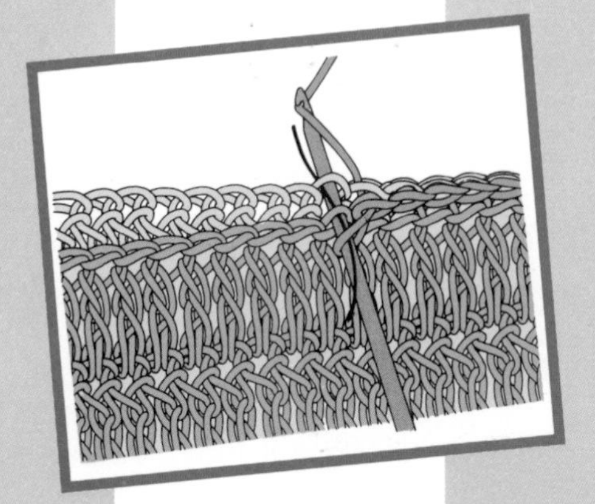

To join invisibly using a crochet hook, place right sides of pieces together and slip stitch through one loop of each piece as illustrated.

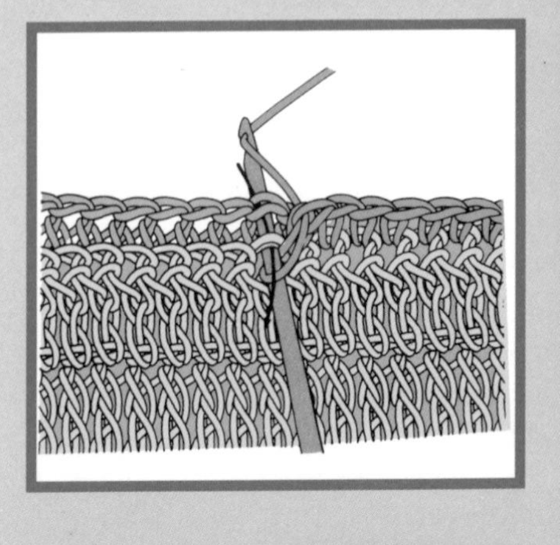

To create a decorative ridged seam on the right side of the work, place wrong sides together and join with double crochet working under two strands of each piece as illustrated.

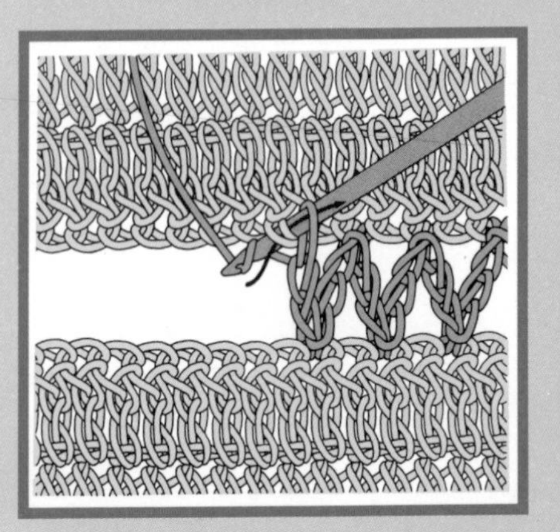

Alternatively with the right side of both pieces uppermost they can be joined with a row of fancy openwork chains.

Abbreviations , Symbols and Terms

Listed below are the standard abbreviations and symbols that have been used in this book. Refer to pages 30 to 47 for more detailed instructions of these and other stitch variations. If a pattern contains an unusual combination of stitches these are explained in the Special Abbreviation at the beginning of that pattern.

Abbreviations

Alt = alternate, **beg** = begin(ning), **ch(s)** = chain(s), **ch sp** = chain space, **cm** = centimetre(s), **dec** = decrease, **dc** = double crochet, **dtr** = double treble, **htr** = half treble, **inc** = increase, **ins** = inches, **quadtr** = quadruple treble, **quintr** = quintuple treble, **rep** = repeat, **sl st** = slip stitch, **sp(s)** = space(s), **st(s)** = stitch(es), **tog** = together, **tr** = treble, **ttr** = triple treble, **yo** = yarn over.

Basic Symbols used in Diagrams

The number of strokes crossing the stems of stitches longer than a half treble represents the number of times the yarn is wrapped over the hook **before** the hook is inserted into the work.

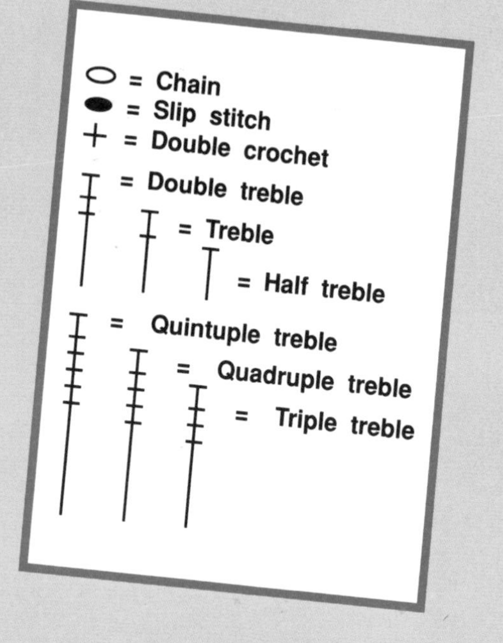

Pattern Terms

Figures or instructions in round brackets ( ) refer to larger sizes.

Figures or instructions in square brackets [ ] should be repeated as stated after the brackets.

The yarn quantities stated are based on average requirements and are therefore approximate.

Top of the Class

Hints and tips to help and improve your crochet.

When working a large piece of crochet it is sensible to start with more chain than necessary as it is simple to undo the extra chain if you have miscounted.

The back and front of crochet stitches are not the same. Stitches worked in rounds usually have the right side facing you all the time, but when working to and fro each side of the fabric may look different. If no right side is indicated with a particular stitch, it is worth making your own decision so that when all pieces are joined, the right sides are matched.

The way you hold the hook can effect your tension. If it is too tight try holding the hook further away from the head of the hook.

To protect large, delicate or lacy items whilst they are being worked it is a good idea to place them in a pillowcase.

Always keep the ball band as a reference, as it usually gives instructions for washing and ironing. The best way is to pin it to the tension swatch and keep it with any left over yarn. That way you can always check the washing instructions and also have materials for repairs.

Working motifs is an ideal way to use up oddments of yarn and very different effects can be achieved by working the same motif in textured yarn and smooth yarn.